Pebble® Plus

Cool Sports Facts

Cool Stock Car Racing Facts

by Sandy Donovan

Consulting Editor: Gail Saunders-Smith, PhD

Consultant: Suzanne Wise, Curator
Stock Car Racing Collection, Appalachian State University Library

CAPSTONE PRESS
a capstone imprint

Pebble Plus is published by Capstone Press,
1710 Roe Crest Drive, North Mankato, Minnesota 56003.
www.capstonepub.com

Books published by Capstone Press are manufactured with paper
containing at least 10 percent post-consumer waste.

Library of Congress Cataloging-in-Publication Data
Donovan, Sandra, 1967–
  Cool stock car racing facts / by Sandy Donovan.
    p. cm. — (Pebble plus. Cool sports facts)
  Includes bibliographical references and index.
  Summary: "Simple text and full-color photos illustrate facts about the history, equipment, and records of stock car
racing"—Provided by publisher.
  ISBN 978-1-4296-5302-2 (library binding)
  ISBN 978-1-4296-6202-4 (paperback)
  1. Stock car racing—Juvenile literature. I. Title. II. Series.
GV1029.9.S74.D73 2011
796.72—dc22   2010028902

Editorial Credits
Katy Kudela, editor; Kyle Grenz, designer; Eric Gohl, media researcher; Laura Manthe, production specialist

Photo Credits
Dreamstime/Lawrence Weslowski Jr., cover; Walter Arce, 15, 17, 21
Getty Images Inc./Dozier Mobley, 13; ISC Archives, 7, 9, 11, 19
Shutterstock/bsankow, 5; Walter G Arce, cover (stock car), back cover, 1

Note to Parents and Teachers

The Cool Sports Facts series supports national social studies standards related to people, places,
and culture. This book describes and illustrates stock car racing. The images support early
readers in understanding the text. The repetition of words and phrases helps early readers learn
new words. This book also introduces early readers to subject-specific vocabulary words, which
are defined in the Glossary section. Early readers may need assistance to read some words and to
use the Table of Contents, Glossary, Read More, Internet Sites, and Index sections of the book.

Printed in the United States of America in North Mankato, Minnesota.
022017   010302R

Table of Contents

Roaring Motors....... 4

Cool History.......... 6

Cool Equipment 14

Cool Records........ 18

Glossary 22

Read More 23

Internet Sites 23

Index 24

Roaring Motors

Engines roar. Crowds cheer.

Stock car racing has many fans.

More than 250 million people

watch these races on

TV each year.

Cool History

In the 1940s stock cars looked like other cars. But watch out! Drivers turned these cars into speed machines when they raced down dirt tracks.

In 1949 Louise Smith's life
changed. She went to watch
a race. But she decided to drive
instead! Smith became the
first lady of racing.

9

It took three days to name
the first Daytona 500 winner.

It was a close race!

Judges finally named

Lee Petty the winner.

The first Daytona 500 was held in 1959.

In a 1987 race, Dale Earnhardt Sr.

found himself off the track.

But he kept driving.

His "pass in the grass"

won him the race.

Cool Equipment

Today stock cars have seats shaped to fit each driver. During a crash the seats keep drivers from bouncing around.

Stock car tires have a

second tire built inside.

If a tire goes flat, a driver

can safely make a pit stop.

Cool Records

In 1977 Janet Guthrie

set a new record.

She was the first woman

to race the Daytona 500.

She took 12th place.

Richard Petty is called "The King."

He has won 200 NASCAR races.

That's 95 more than

any other driver!

Glossary

Daytona 500—the first race of NASCAR's Cup season; it is held at the Daytona International Speedway in Florida

NASCAR—National Association for Stock Car Auto Racing

pit stop—a break drivers take from the race so the pit crew can add fuel, change tires, and make repairs to a car

record—when something is done first or better than anyone has ever done it before

stock car—the first stock cars were regular cars anyone could buy; today stock cars look like regular cars but are changed a lot to allow for super-fast, safe racing

Read More

Doeden, Matt. *Stock Cars.* Mighty Machines. Mankato, Minn.: Capstone Press, 2007.

Riggs, Kate. *Stock Cars.* Now That's Fast! Mankato, Minn.: Creative Education, 2010.

Internet Sites

FactHound offers a safe, fun way to find Internet sites related to this book. All of the sites on FactHound have been researched by our staff.

Here's all you do:

Visit *www.facthound.com*

Type in this code: 9781429653022

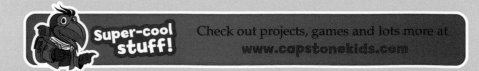

Super-cool stuff! Check out projects, games and lots more at www.capstonekids.com

Index

crashes, 14

Daytona 500, 10, 18

Earnhardt, Dale, Sr., 12

fans, 4

Guthrie, Janet, 18

Petty, Lee, 10

Petty, Richard, 20

pit stops, 16

seats, 14

Smith, Louise, 8

tires, 16

tracks, 6, 12

Word Count: 203

Grade: 1

Early-Intervention Level: 20